Cooking Up some AMERICAN HISTORY

Sunflower

education

Exceptional Books for Teachers and Parents

A Great Way to Teach American History!

Finally, authentic historical recipes designed for classroom use! Turn children's love of food into a love of American history. This unique cookbook provides authentic recipes in historical contexts, adding flavor to learning.

Combine cooking and eating with new information and you have the perfect recipe for retention. A lesson about the Civil War is a lot more memorable if you do it while nibbling on some authentic hardtack!

Recipes are historically accurate. There is a nice mix of snacks, entrees, and even desserts. Want to know what George Washington's favorite breakfast was? Or what wealthy Spanish colonists ate for a treat? The answers and actual recipes are right here!

Grades 2 and Up • 50 Complete, Authentic, Kid-friendly Recipes

Printed to Fit 4 x 6 Recipe Cards

Companion book to *Cooking Up Some World History!*

Please feel free to photocopy the sheets in this book within reason. Sunflower Education grants teachers permission to photocopy the sheets from this book for educational use. This permission is granted to individual teachers and not entire schools or school systems. Please send any permissions questions to permissions@SunflowerEducation.net.

DISCLAIMER: THIS COOKBOOK IS FOR ADULTS ONLY. Cooking and eating are inherently hazardous. Your use of this book constitutes an agreement to hold Sunflower Education and its affiliates harmless for any adverse effects that may or may not arise from the use of the recipes in this book. Some recipes may contain ingredients dangerous to people with food allergies. Use only high quality ingredients. Follow all safety rules.

Visit **SunflowerEducation.Net** for more great books!

Editorial   Sunflower Education

Design   Blue Agave Studio

ISBN-13: 978-1-937166-07-6
ISBN-10: 1-937166-07-4
Copyright © 2011
Sunflower Education
All rights reserved.
Printed in the U.S.A.

Contents

To the Teacher

Every kid loves to eat!

Cooking Up Some American History gives you a way to turn children's love of food into a love of American history. It is a unique cookbook that provides truly authentic recipes in historical contexts, adding flavor to learning.

Cooking and Eating: Good Pedagogy

We all know that food is a necessary and enjoyable part of life. But did you know that there are countless learning opportunities wrapped up in every meal? Get your students hooked on history with this delicious, interdisciplinary approach. Read on to see all the different ways students can learn from a more culinary classroom.

Cooking . . . Increases Retention

Cooking and eating stimulate all the senses. Couple this stimulation with new information and you have the perfect recipe for retention. A lesson about the Civil War, for example, is a lot more memorable if you complete it while nibbling on some hardtack. For decades, studies have established the link between multi-sensual stimulation and learning. Think back for a minute: don't some of your most memorable lessons involve hands-on activities?

Cooking . . . is Interdisciplinary

Just as food can unite different kinds of people around one table, so too can it reach across disciplines. Cooking is one of the most interdisciplinary activities in which a child can take part. Here is a list of a few of the topics covered by cooking and eating.

- **Math** When children cook, they don't just learn what a measurement symbol is, they get a real idea of how big a cup is compared to a pint. Basic addition and division are a must as students measure and count how much of each ingredient they need. Students even get to see fractions in action when slicing a cake into enough pieces for everyone. Different clocks and timers can be used to keep track of time.

- **Science** Cooking is chemistry in action. Students get to see chemical reactions occur right before their eyes when dough rises, for example. By measuring and following recipes, children begin to learn the skills they will need for scientific experiments. When learning about seasonal foods, students can see the effects of the seasons throughout a school year.

- **Language Arts** By learning about different times in American history and about different ways of life, students will expand their vocabularies. They will learn to be careful readers because reading the recipe closely will make the dish as tasty as possible. Finally, students will become aware that cooking is one of the ways in which people express themselves. They will see a meal as a story, just like a story in a book.

- **Social Studies** These recipes will make history more tangible for your students. They will gain first-hand experience of what life was like for Americans in earlier times. They will also be able to appreciate the many different cultures whose creativity and tenacity made America what it is today: a melting pot.

Cooking . . . is Healthy!

Cooking and cleaning are real-world skills that everyone needs to know. Preparing meals for yourself is almost always healthier than eating at a restaurant or grabbing some fast food. Being able to safely prepare and store food opens a whole new world of meal possibilities throughout life.

Cooking . . . Encourages Critical Thinking

When you are cooking with your class, encourage students to ask questions as the recipe unfolds. This way, everyone can learn about the different parts of a recipe. If something goes wrong, engage the class, asking them how it could be fixed. This critical thinking will help foster early problem-solving skills and give students a sense of ownership in what they make.

The Experts Agree!

The United States Department of Agriculture has stated, "kitchen tasks give your child a chance to measure, count, and see food change. That's early math and science learning. Your child can learn new words and symbols by cooking with you. Talk about the food and what you are doing. Read words together on food containers. Small muscle skills develop, too, when your child uses his or her hands to help with kitchen tasks."

The Department of Agriculture has even acknowledged how cooking can help to build students' self esteem. Cooking lets them see in a very real way the fruits of their labors, and students can gain a real sense of pride when they grade their own work by how great it tastes!

How to Use This Book

Of course you know how to use a cookbook! Here are some ideas for integrating the cooking (and the eating!) with learning.

Safety First

Please study, follow, and communicate to your students the importance of safety around food. It's not just sharp knives and hot stoves that can cause harm. You should also consider food allergies, choking hazards, and a multitude of other potential dangers. Please study and follow the provided Food and Drug Administration and Department of Agriculture food safety rules and tips—and make sure children do the same.

Permission

Parents and guardians are keenly aware of what their children consume—and rightfully so. Be aware of food allergies and other dietary restrictions. Be sure to follow your school policies and use the provided permission slips.

Cooking, Eating, or Both?

One of the criteria used to determine what recipes to include in this cookbook was ease of preparation. Recipes include relatively few ingredients and are relatively easy to prepare. Thus, the recipes are ideal to prepare with children. If you are in a position to cook with children, be sure to make safety your first priority. Or, of course, you may prepare dishes yourself and bring them to class as a learning treat.

Suggested Lesson Cycle

Using this general outline as a basis for lessons will yield good results.

- **Appetizer (Introduce)** Tell students that they are going to be learning about a certain place, time, event, or people in American history. Remind them that, although removed in time, the people of history were very much like people today—right down to getting hungry! Ask: *What do you think the people of this time ate? How did they get their food? Why do you think that?*

  As appropriate, read aloud or summarize the relevant summary page (e.g., Native American Foods, Spanish Colonial Fare, etc.) and use it to focus the discussion. Tell students the name of the specific dish you will cook or eat.

- **Main Course (Teach)** Each recipe is accompanied by an introduction. As appropriate, share the information with students. Each recipe is also accompanied by a Classroom Connection. Most of these are short, simple, fun activities of various levels of difficulty that connect the recipe to history, math, science, or the language arts. A few are longer research tasks. As appropriate, assign them to students.

- **Dessert (close)** Above all help students make meaning. Cooking and eating historical foods are valuable educational activities in and of themselves, but the icing on the cake is when students connect the food to an academic and empathetic understanding and feeling of American history.

Vegetarian Dishes

Many kinds of meat have played a vital role in the American diet. For ease of preparation and food safety issues (for example, the risk of cross-contamination), all of the recipes provided in this cookbook are vegetarian. This is a feature requested by many teachers.

A Note on Authenticity

The recipes in *Cooking Up Some American History* are the real deal. A great amount of research was conducted to ensure their historical accuracy. Occasional, very minor alterations to accommodate modern realities should have no effect on your being able to share true tastes of the past with your students.

Please note that *Cooking Up Some American History* is not intended as a comprehensive treatment of American food history—a fascinating yet remarkably complex topic. What it does provide are authentic and representative dishes from major periods of American history. These recipes will thrill your students, each of whom will be delighted to say, "I ate the same food they did!"

Have fun and happy cooking!

Kitchen & Safety Rules from the Food and Drug Administration

❶ Clean The first rule of safe food preparation is to keep everything clean.

- Wash hands with warm water and soap for 20 seconds before and after handling any food. For children, this means the time it takes to sing "Happy Birthday" twice.

- Wash surfaces (cutting boards, dishes, utensils, countertops) with hot, soapy water after preparing each food item and before going on to the next item.

- Rinse fruits and vegetables thoroughly under cool running water and use a produce brush to remove surface dirt.

- Do not rinse raw meat and poultry before cooking. "Washing these foods makes it more likely for bacteria to spread to areas around the sink and countertops," says Marjorie Davidson of the FDA.

❷ Separate Don't give bacteria the opportunity to spread from one food to another (cross-contamination).

- Keep egg products, raw meat, poultry, seafood, and their juices away from foods that won't be cooked. Take this precaution while shopping in the store, when storing in the refrigerator at home, and while preparing meals.

- Consider using one cutting board only for foods that will be cooked (such as raw meat, poultry, and seafood) and another one for those that will not be cooked (such as raw fruits and vegetables).

- Keep fruits and vegetables that will be eaten raw separate from other foods such as raw meat, poultry or seafood—and from kitchen utensils used for those products.

- Do not put cooked meat or other food that is ready to eat on an unwashed plate that has held any egg products, or any raw meat, poultry, seafood, or their juices.

❸ Cook Food is safely cooked when it reaches an internal temperature that is high enough to kill harmful bacteria.

- "Color is not a reliable indicator of doneness," says Davidson. Use a food thermometer to make sure meat, poultry, and fish are cooked to a safe internal temperature. To check a turkey for safety, for example, insert a food thermometer into the innermost part of the thigh and wing and the thickest part of the breast. The turkey is safe when the temperature reaches 165°F. If the turkey is stuffed, the temperature of the stuffing should be 165°F.

- Bring sauces, soups, and gravies to a rolling boil when reheating.
- Cook eggs until the yolk and white are firm. When making your own eggnog or other recipe calling for raw eggs, use pasteurized shell eggs, liquid or frozen pasteurized egg products, or powdered egg whites.
- Don't eat uncooked cookie dough, which may contain raw eggs.

❹ Chill Refrigerate foods quickly because harmful bacteria grow rapidly at room temperature.

- Refrigerate leftovers and takeout foods—and *any* type of food that should be refrigerated—within two hours.
- Set your refrigerator at or below 40°F and the freezer at 0°F. Check both periodically with an appliance thermometer.
- Never defrost food at room temperature. Food can be defrosted safely in the refrigerator, under cold running water, or in the microwave. Food thawed in cold water or in the microwave should be cooked immediately.
- Allow the correct amount of time to properly thaw food. For example, a 20-pound turkey needs four to five days to thaw completely when thawed in the refrigerator.
- Don't taste food that looks or smells questionable. Davidson says, "a good rule to follow is, when in doubt, throw it out."
- Leftovers should be used within three to four days.

Cooking Safety Tips from the Department of Agriculture

- Fasten hair back if it's long.
- Wear clean clothes.
- Get started by washing hands and tables.
- Taste with a clean spoon. A licked spoon goes in the sink, not back in the bowl.
- Resist nibbling cookie dough or cake batter.
- Have children stay away from hot surfaces, utensils, and sharp objects. An adult needs to help.
- Work at a table or child-size surface.
- Walk slowly. Carry food and utensils with care.
- Wipe up spills.

Cooking Up Some History!
Food Tasting Permission Slip

Dear Parent or Guardian,

In order to enhance our study of history and culture, we will be tasting an authentic food in class. It is important to know if your child has any food allergies or intolerances that will prevent her/him from participating in this activity.

Please complete the form below and have your child bring it to class by _____.

Student's Name: _____

Food Allergies or Dietary Restrictions

Please check one of the following:

☐ My child DOES NOT have a food allergy or dietary restriction.

☐ My child DOES have a food allergy or dietary restriction(s). (*Please identify on back.*)

Permission to Participate in Tasting

☐ My child DOES have permission to participate in the food tasting.

☐ My child DOES NOT have permission to participate in the food tasting.

Signature _____ Date _____

Cooking Up Some History!
Food Preparation Permission Slip

Dear Parent or Guardian,

In order to enhance our study of history and culture, we will be making an authentic food in class. Students will be asked to perform age-appropriate kitchen tasks. They will be taught safety rules and closely monitored at all times.

Please complete the form below and have your child bring it to class by _____.

Student's Name: _____

Permission to Participate in Food Preparation

Please check one of the following:

☐ My child DOES have permission to participate in food preparation.

☐ My child DOES NOT have permission to participate in food preparation.

Signature _____ Date _____

～ Classroom Safety Signs ～

Safety is the top priority when cooking with and feeding children. An environment consciously designed to promote safety is a proven method to reduce accidents and injuries. The signs on the following pages will help you create such an environment.

Please feel free to copy the pages (onto colored paper to attract greater attention) and post them where you will be cooking and eating with children.

Call students' attention to each sign in turn. Have the students read the sign aloud, explain what it means, and give examples. Share scenarios of when each sign would be applicable and have the students describe appropriate responses.

Safety First!

Follow the Rules!

Wash Your Hands!

CookingUpHistory.com

Ask for Help!

CookingUpHistory.com

Clean Up!

Cooking Up Some American History

It's OK to Make a Little Mess!

Help Each Other!

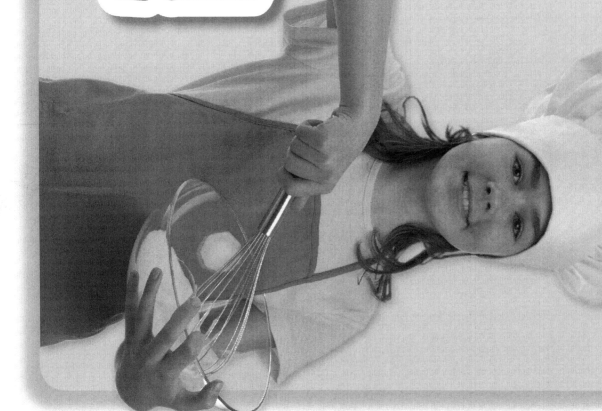

Focus On What You Are Doing!

Cooking Up Some American History

CookingUpHistory.com

Native American Foods

Long before Europeans came to the New World, Native Americans feasted on an abundance of wild game and plants. Deer and buffalo were plentiful, as were fish in the streams and oceans. There was a multitude of roots, berries, fruits, and vegetables. The land fed millions, for millennia. Native Americans were experts at using what the land provided.

Many Native Americans were also skilled farmers, growing crops that helped sustain their tribes through the winter. The practice of growing corn, beans, and squash together, known as the "Three Sisters," is a good example of Native American agriculture ingenuity. The corn grows tall to support the beans and the squash covers the ground to hold water and prevent weeds. The three work together to help each other grow.

Native Americans shared their food and food-getting skills with the colonists; generosity that allowed the newcomers to survive in the New World.

Banaha
A Native American Staple

Corn was a staple, or major source of food, for many Native American groups. Most cooked a version of this simple bread made from cornmeal. This particular recipe is from the Choctaw.

Classroom Connection For centuries, the Choctaw lived in what is now Mississippi and Alabama. They were primarily farmers who augmented their diet by hunting. One of their most important religious ceremonies was called the Green Corn Dance. They held the celebration at harvest time. What can you conclude from this? *[That corn was extremely important, and even sacred, to the Choctaw people.]*

CookingUpHistory.com

Banaha

2 cups of cornmeal	1 teaspoon salt
1 ½ cups hot water	Corn shucks (boil about 10 minutes before using)
1 teaspoon soda	

Combine the dry ingredients. Add the hot water and then mix until the dough is firm enough to handle easily. Mold balls of dough about the size of a tennis ball and wrap them in cornhusks. Tie them in the middle with corn shuck string. Drop the wrapped balls into a pot of boiling water deep enough for all the balls to submerge. Cover and cook 40 minutes. Serve. Refrigerate any leftovers. To serve, cut ½ inch thick slices and fry them in hot oil fat. [2 ½ loaves]

Succotash
Cooking with the "Three Sisters"

Often referred to as the "Three Sisters," squash, corn, and beans were raised together by many Native American groups. Not only do the three crops help each other grow, they come together to make a delicious and very nutritious meal. Succotash is made using the Three Sisters.

Classroom Connection Indians of Mesoamerican often grew the Three Sisters together in fields called "milpas." Milpas are marvels of productivity and soil conservation. If a one-acre milpa could feed a family of five, how many acres of milpas would be needed to feed a village of 240 people? [48]

Succotash

CookingUpHistory.com

1 butternut squash, washed
2 cans of corn
1 10 oz. package frozen lima beans

Butter
Salt & Pepper

Scoop out the seeds from the squash then cut the squash into small pieces. Remove the peel from the pieces and place them into a pot. Add enough water to cover all the pieces. Bring the water to a boil, reduce the heat, cover, and simmer until the squash is tender, about 30 minutes. Add the corn and lima beans to the pot. Simmer until the corn and beans are tender, about 15 minutes. Drain the water from the mixture. Toss the succotash with salt, pepper, and butter.

Toasted Pumpkin Seeds
Waste Not, Want Not

Native Americans were well known for making efficient use of their food resources. Using the seeds from pumpkins is a powerful demonstration of this vital survival skill.

Classroom Connection Why is it important to not waste food? Why might it have been especially important for people hundreds and thousands of years ago to not waste food? *[Answers will vary. Food is a precious resource. Long ago, more effort was required to obtain food, and it was not as abundant.]*

CookingUpHistory.com

Toasted Pumpkin Seeds
pumpkin seeds (scooped, cleaned, and washed)

oil

salt

Spread seeds in one layer on a baking sheet. Brush lightly with oil. Season with salt (or dried herbs). Bake at 350 degrees until the seeds are lightly browned.

Spanish Colonial Fare

The Spanish were among the first European explorers of the New World and the first Europeans to taste traditional Central and South American foods that combine chiles, tomatoes, and spices. As they colonized the Americas, the Spanish eagerly explored the new foods available to them, eating the same dishes as the natives.

The Spanish shared these exciting foods with Europe. In fact, many of the things we eat today that are associated with European nations actually came from the Americas. Swiss chocolate, Irish potatoes, and French vanilla are all plants that originated in Central and South America. The Spanish colonists not only found new territory, they discovered a whole new menu.

Butter Wafers
A Sweet Treat

Butter and sugar were rare items in the colonies and only available to the wealthy. With the addition of the native vanilla, these cookie-like wafers were a Spanish delicacy.

Classroom Connection Butter Wafers were a delicacy. So only the richest people would be able to eat them, and they might only have them on special occasions. What are some foods that you only eat on special occasions? *[Answers will vary. Ensure students are respectful of one another's traditions.]*

CookingUpHistory.com

Butter Wafers

½ cup butter
½ cup vegetable shortening
1 ½ teaspoons grated lemon peel
1 teaspoon vanilla extract

1 ¼ cups sugar
2 eggs
1 ¾ cups flour
½ teaspoon salt

Cream the butter and vegetable shortening with lemon peel and vanilla extract. Add the sugar gradually, beating until fluffy. Continue beating thoroughly as you add the eggs one at a time. Mix the flour and salt; add to creamed mixture in thirds, mixing until blended after each addition. Cool the dough in a refrigerator until easy to handle. Removing a small portion of dough at a time, shape into ¾ to 1 inch balls and place 1 ½ inches apart on an ungreased cookie sheet. Bake at 350 degrees for 8 to 10 minutes.

Salsa
Feel the Rhythm!

Tomatoes, chiles, and spices were standard fare for the natives of Central America. Spaniard Alonso de Molina first named the combination "salsa" in 1571.

Classroom Connection In Spanish, "salsa" means sauce, so Alonso de Molina was calling Salsa a sauce. Pick out four different foods or items in the kitchen and look up what they are called in Spanish. *[Answers will vary. An English-Spanish dictionary or online translator can be used to verify student answers.]*

Salsa

CookingUpHistory.com

2-3 tomatoes, diced

1 onion, diced

1 poblano or jalapeno chili pepper, diced small

salt

cilantro, chopped fine

Mix the chopped tomatoes, onions and chili (if desired include more of any ingredient). Season to taste with salt and cilantro.

Corn Tortillas
It's a Wrap!

Corn forms the basis for many South and Central American foods. The most basic and famous of these is the tortilla.

Classroom Connection How many tacos can you eat in one meal? The world record for most tacos eaten in 11 minutes is 48. How many tacos did the record-breaker eat per minute? *[an average of 4.36]* Why is eating like this dangerous? *[a person could choke or get sick]*

CookingUpHistory.com

Corn Tortillas
2 cups Masa Harina
1 ¼ to 1 ⅓ cups water

Combine the Masa Harina and 1 ¼ cup of water; knead to form masa (dough); if too dry, add more water 1 teaspoon at a time. Be careful to not over or under moisten the masa. Keep covered when not in use. Roll a golf-ball sized ball. Press it in a tortilla press. *Without a tortilla press:* Set the masa between two pieces of plastic. Roll out into a 6" round tortilla. Transfer the tortilla to a hot, dry skillet. Cook for about 30 seconds on one side; gently flip over. Cook for about 60 seconds (it should puff a little); flip back to the first side. Cook for another 30 seconds on the first side.

English Colonial Dishes

English colonists benefited greatly from Native Americans, who taught the colonists how to survive in the New World and how to cook new foods, such as corn. Still, the colonists brought with them many traditional foods and recipes. As the colonies prospered and grew, people brought even more recipes and traditions from the Old World.

While they adapted their recipes to include the foods of the New World, the dishes closely resembled the same dishes from home. The colonists brought their own fruits and vegetables to plant in the New World and continued to use them in their cooking.

The colonists brought their European recipes. The New World provided interesting new ingredients. The Native Americans taught skills and techniques. All of these things combined to create a new and distinct tradition of food; a perfect companion to the new and distinct country that was forming.

Rock Candy
A Bit of Crystallized Goodness

Sugar was a luxury for the early colonists, but when it was available it was put to good use. Sweet confections were popular with all of the peoples living in the New World.

Classroom Connection When we make rock candy, we are actually crystallizing sugar molecules. The shapes that they take are determined by the nature of sugar molecules. Try the recipe again using salt instead of sugar. What shapes do the salt crystals make compared with the sugar crystals? *[Salt forms cube-shaped crystals.]*

CookingUpHistory.com

Rock Candy

4 ½ cup sugar

2 cups water

4 12 oz. glass jars, sterilized

4 7-inch pieces clean string

4 wooden skewers or pencils

food coloring

Tie one end of each string around the center of a pencil. Place 1 string in each jar, resting the pencil across the rim of the jar. Trim the strings to ensure they do not touch the bottoms of the jars. Mix the sugar into the water in a saucepan. Bring the sugar water to boil over medium-high heat, stirring occasionally; boil, stirring occasionally, for 5 minutes. Remove from heat. Add food coloring. Let the syrup stand 5 minutes. Pour about 1 cup syrup into each jar. Loosely cover with pierced aluminum foil. Let stand for 2 weeks or until crystals form on strings. (Every few days break up hard sugar layer on surface.) Remove strings from jars and suspend until crystals are dry (about 1 hour).

Shrewsbury Cakes
Cookie, Cake, or Both?

George Bernard Shaw said, "England and America are two countries separated by the same language." Brought to the New World from England, Shrewsbury Cakes look a lot more like what Americans think of as cookies.

Classroom Connection Another example of how people in England and America have different words for the same thing is what Americans call the trunk of a car. The English call it a boot. Try to find the English equivalent for the American words *apartment, elevator, soccer,* and *french fries.* [*flat, lift, football,* and *chips*]

Shrewsbury Cakes

CookingUpHistory.com

½ cup butter	½ cup flour
½ cup sugar	½ teaspoon nutmeg
1 egg	

Preheat the oven to 350 degrees. Grease a cookie sheet. Cream the butter and sugar. Add the egg and mix until well blended. Stir in the flour and nutmeg, mix until batter is smooth. Place a teaspoon of batter on cookie sheets, 2 inches apart from each other. Bake for 10 minutes or until the edges turn brown.

Pea Soup
When Old Meets New

A recipe originally from England, this soup combines an Old World ingredient, peas, with a New World ingredient, potatoes.

Classroom Connection Make a list of the ingredients for Pea Soup. How much of each ingredient would you need if you wanted to triple the amount of soup? *[12 cups dried English peas; 12 quarts water; 18 peppercorns; 6 cloves garlic, chopped; 3 large onions, chopped; 6-9 potatoes, chopped; salt as needed; 3 tablespoons sage; 3 tablespoons thyme; 6 tablespoons lovage (parsley)]*

CookingUpHistory.com

Pea Soup

4 cups dried English peas
4 quarts water
6 peppercorns
2 cloves garlic, chopped
1 large onion, chopped
2-3 potatoes, chopped

salt as needed
1 tablespoon sage
1 tablespoon thyme
2 tablespoons lovage (parsley)

Add the peas, water, and seasonings to a pot. Bring the water to a boil and skim off any foam that rises to the top. Simmer until almost done (possibly several hours). Add the potatoes. Cook until the potatoes are soft. Add more water if the peas start to stick to the pot.

Foods of the Revolutionary War

During the Revolutionary War, the growing, gathering, and hunting of food remained vital activities. Farmers grew vegetables and grains. Root vegetables such as potatoes were popular because they were easily stored. Grains, like wheat and barley, were used for breads and ale. Pickling and preserving were common in an effort to store enough food for the winter. Domesticated animals were also a part of most households. Most men would spend time hunting wild game and fishing.

Many communities continued to share afternoon meals, as the early colonists did, in order to stretch the available food. This was also an opportunity to share news about the war.

Of course, food had to be made available for soldiers. General George Washington estimated that 20 million pounds of meat and 100 thousand barrels of flour were needed to feed 15 thousand soldiers.

A soldier's rations typically included flour or cornmeal, some sort of salted meat, and beans. The men were expected to cook their own food, which usually meant a stew-like dish cooked until the beans were soft. Occasionally they were able to forage for berries and herbs to liven up the dish.

Hasty Pudding
A Quick Fix

A popular dish that stretched the available foods—often in short supply during wartime—as well as using local ingredients like maple sugar and molasses.

Classroom Connection The milk, cream, and maple syrup for this recipe are measured in cups. Convert these measurements into pints and then quarts. *[1 pint or ½ quart of milk; 1 pint or ½ quart of cream; ¼ pint or ⅛ quart of maple syrup]*

CookingUpHistory.com

Hasty Pudding

2 cups milk	½ cup maple syrup (molasses)	⅛ teaspoon nutmeg
2 cups cream	1 tablespoon butter	pinch of ground cloves
3 tablespoons stone ground yellow cornmeal	1 teaspoon cinnamon	⅛ teaspoon baking soda
½ cup brown sugar (maple sugar)	1 teaspoon ginger	2 eggs, beaten
	½ teaspoon salt	

In a heavy pan, scald the milk and cream. Slowly add the yellow cornmeal and bring to a boil, stirring briskly. Stir in sugar, maple syrup, butter and all the other dry ingredients. Let the mixture cool slightly. In a small bowl, beat the eggs with the milk/cream mixture. Pour the batter into a buttered 1½ quart baking dish and bake at 325 degrees for 2 hours. Serve hot or warm with whipped cream or ice cream.

Firecake
Get It While It's Hot!

When rations were low, Firecake was distributed in an effort to stretch supplies and keep the flour from spoiling.

Classroom Connection Imagine what it must have been like for soldiers in the American Revolution when supplies were low. What would it have been like marching for miles a day with nothing to eat but Firecake and water? *[Answers will vary. Reward thoughtful responses.]*

Firecake   CookingUpHistory.com
Flour
Salt
Water

Add a little salt to flour and mix. Add enough water to make a thick, damp dough. Take a handful and mold into a flat cake. Place the cakes on a cookie sheet and bake until brown.

HoeCakes/ Mushcakes
Washington's Favorite

This was George Washington's favorite breakfast! He would drown them in honey and butter and down them with his usual three cups of tea.

Classroom Connection Most of the ingredients for George Washington's HoeCakes came from his land. Look on the packaging for your favorite breakfast. Where did the ingredients for it come from? What do you make of this? *[Answers will vary. People today eat vastly greater amounts of processed and packaged foods and foods from far away.]*

CookingUpHistory.com

Hoecakes/Mushcakes

8 ¾ cups cornmeal	warm water
1 ¼ teaspoons dry yeast	shortening or other cooking grease
1 egg	honey & butter

Combine 4 cups of cornmeal, 1 ¼ teaspoons of dry yeast and 3 ½ cups of warm water. Cover and set on the stove or counter overnight. In the morning, slowly add the remaining cornmeal, egg, and enough warm water to give the mixture the consistency of pancake batter (3-4 cups). Cover and set aside for 20 minutes. Grease a griddle or skillet and heat until water sprinkled on it will bead up. Spoon the batter onto the griddle. When the one side of the hoecake browns, flip it over and brown the other side. Serve warm with butter and honey.

Dining in Young America

After the Revolutionary War, the United States was a new nation and its citizens soon developed their own identity. Language, art, and literature took on a distinctly American character. Americans began their own food traditions as well. *American Cookery* (1796) by Amelia Simmons is a perfect example. This was the first cookbook written by an American for Americans. It used ingredients that were uniquely American, such as turkey, squash, potatoes, and cranberries.

Along with perfecting new dishes, Americans began new traditions in the way they ate. Elaborate dinner parties, with numerous courses served, often lasted for hours. Strict table manners were expected to be followed. Numerous etiquette guides were published to help.

These meals were even more extravagant for the holidays, especially Thanksgiving. Although not yet a national holiday, Americans celebrated the event with large amounts of food. Family members would join together for a day of eating, entertaining, and enjoying one another.

The discovery of pearl ash in the late 1700s changed baking in the United States and around the world. In the past, breads were made with yeast and then time was spent letting the dough rise; a process that adds air to the dough to create softness. Pearl ash did the same thing to bread, only without the lengthy process of letting the bread rise. This was the forerunner of modern day baking powder, and it revolutionized baking.

Jumbles
The Original Doughnuts

This dish is the early American version of what became pretzels, bagels, and doughnuts. Although this recipe calls for baking, many others of the time said to boil the jumbles, like our modern doughnuts.

Classroom Connection If all of the ingredients for these jumbles cost $6.43, how many dollars, quarters, dimes, nickels, and pennies would you need in order to get to that amount? *[6 dollars, 1 quarter, 1 dime, 1 nickel, and 3 pennies]*

CookingUpHistory.com

Jumbles

2 cups soft butter	2 teaspoons ginger
2 cups white sugar	3 medium eggs
2 teaspoons nutmeg	6 cups flour
2 teaspoons cinnamon	

Mix the butter and sugar, cream them until they have a very light consistency. Mix in the nutmeg, cinnamon, and ginger. Whisk the eggs to a pale yellow cream. Blend the eggs with the butter and sugar mixture. Sift the flour. Add it to the mixture one cup at a time until a soft but not sticky ball of dough is formed. Use a rolling pin to flatten the dough on a floured surface to about ¼ inch thickness. Slice pieces off with a knife, roll them with your fingertips into ropes about ¾ inches in diameter. Twist two ropes together and form into a 6 inch ring. Bake at 350 degrees for 12-15 minutes.

Popcorn
Gotta Love that Sound!

Popcorn was a favorite of the Native Americans and soon became a favorite of all Americans. It was especially popular during long dinner parties as a way to entertain children.

Classroom Connection Take a handful of popcorn. Arrange the pieces into a square, a rectangle, a triangle, a circle, and then a hexagon. *[Observe students making the shapes individually or in small groups.]*

Popcorn

CookingUpHistory.com

2 to 3 tablespoons of vegetable oil
1 cup popcorn kernels
salt to taste
melted butter to taste

Spread vegetable oil inside a large, heavy stock pot. Place a couple of popcorn kernels in the pot. When the test kernels pop, add the remaining popcorn. Cover, and continuously shake pot side-to-side, allowing the heat to spread to all the kernels. Listen to the time between pops. When time between pops becomes one to two seconds long, remove pot from heat. Cool slightly, then pour into a bowl. Add salt and butter to taste.

Pumpkin Bread
An Autumnal Treat

A delicious example of a "quick bread"—a bread made with baking powder instead of yeast—just like early Americans used pearl ash. The pumpkin makes it especially American!

Classroom Connection Pumpkins are strongly associated with America. What American holidays do pumpkins play an important part of? In what way? *[Thanksgiving pumpkin pie and Halloween jack-o'-lanterns]*

CookingUpHistory.com

Pumpkin Bread

3 cups sugar	3 ½ cups flour	1 teaspoon allspice
1 cup vegetable oil	2 teaspoons salt	1 teaspoon cinnamon
4 eggs, lightly beaten	2 teaspoons baking soda	½ teaspoon cloves
16 ounces canned	1 teaspoon baking powder	⅔ cups water
unsweetened pumpkin	1 teaspoon nutmeg	

Preheat oven to 350 degrees. Butter and flour 2 9x5 loaf pans. Combine the sugar and oil. Stir in the eggs and pumpkin. Mix the dry ingredients in a separate bowl. Blend the dry ingredients and water into wet mixture. Split the batter between two loaf pans. Bake for 30-40 minutes or until cake tester comes out clean. Let stand 10 minutes. Remove from pans and cool.

Staying Fed
on the Frontier

As the country grew, people continued to move west, exploring and settling new territory. The pioneers' journeys were long and dull, especially where food was concerned. Everything on the journey had to be portable, which meant there was a lot of dried food. Pioneers ate dried meat like salt pork and beef jerky. These were accompanied by dried beans, flour, cornmeal, and rice. There was not much variety on a journey that could be as long as 2,000 miles.

Once the pioneers were settled on their claim, they spent long hours producing food. Unlike people back east, pioneers had no local market at which to shop. The main activity of a pioneer's life was to grow, gather, or hunt food and then preserve it to last through the long winter months.

Kitchen gardens were necessary for many households' survival. They would grow all the vegetables for the family. As the vegetables became ripe, they were immediately dried or made into preserves so they would last. Gardens were not easy to maintain; along with weeds and the need for water, pioneers had to fight to keep gophers, crows, deer, and even bears out of the garden.

Meat was also difficult to provide. Once the meat was brought in, it had to be preserved quickly. This was usually done by salting or smoking—both lengthy and difficult processes. Only in winter was preserving the meat easy; it could be stored outside where it would freeze.

Hard work, willingness to improvise, and sheer determination enabled the pioneers to feed themselves.

Journey Potatoes
In for the Long Haul

A hearty dish that uses kitchen garden staples: potatoes and onions. Encourage students to bring in vegetables from gardens at their homes.

Classroom Connection What if next year your whole school got together for Thanksgiving and your class had to make enough Journey Potatoes for everyone? You would need a lot of potatoes! If you needed 60 potatoes for everyone, you would have a fair bit of counting to do. Skip count by 2's to 10, and then skip count by 5's up to 60. *[2, 4, 6, 8, 10, 15, 20, 25, 30, 35, 40, 45, 50, 55, 60]*

CookingUpHistory.com

Journey Potatoes

2 pounds potatoes

¼ pound onion

1 teaspoon salt

2 cups milk

Peel the potatoes. Cut into thin slices. Cut the onion into thin slices. Fill a pot with the potatoes, onion, and salt. Cover them in water and bring to a boil. Boil for 3 minutes. Remove from heat and add milk. Return to heat and let simmer until heated through.

Peach Leather
No . . . Not That Kind of Leather!

Any fruit that was gathered had to be preserved. Drying fruit into a "leather" was a simple and effective preservation technique.

Classroom Connection What happened when you left the Peach Leather out to dry in the sun? The water in the peaches evaporated. List the three physical states of water. What are the words for when water goes from solid to liquid? Liquid to solid? Liquid to gas? And gas to liquid? *[Solid (ice), liquid (water), gas (steam); melting; freezing; evaporating or boiling; condensing.]*

Peach Leather

CookingUpHistory.com

1 pound peeled, stoned peaches
½ cup sugar
oil
muslin

Place the sugar and peaches in a heavy pot of water. Bring slowly to a boil. Simmer until most of the moisture has cooked away, mashing to a smooth paste as they cook. Lightly oil a platter and cover it with muslin. Cover the platter with a thin layer of the mashed peaches. Let dry in the sun, then roll in the cloth and store in a cool, dry place. To eat, unroll and tear off pieces.

Scalloped Tomatoes
Layers and Layers of "Yum"

Any food that wasn't preserved had to be eaten quickly. This dish is a good example of how fresh vegetables were used.

Classroom Connection This recipe calls for ripe tomatoes. While picking them out at the grocery store, you find one ripe tomato out of every three that you pick up. How many tomatoes will you have to examine to get 8 ripe tomatoes? *[24]*

CookingUpHistory.com

Scalloped Tomatoes

Ripe tomatoes

Buttered bread crumbs

Salt and pepper

Pare and slice the tomatoes. Alternate layers of tomato and bread crumbs in a baking dish. Season each layer with salt and pepper. Cover the dish and bake until very hot and the top layer of crumbs is brown.

 Foods Out of Africa

The men and women brought to America from Africa did not come willingly. They were kidnapped, enslaved, and shipped to the New World where they faced lifetimes of abuse and work.

Most slaves were given a paltry monthly allowance of food. Eight pounds of pork or dried fish and one bushel of cornmeal was typical. Any other food they had to provide themselves, after their forced labor was finished.

Some enslaved Africans were given small patches of land to grow their own vegetables. They caught their own meat when they could by trapping and fishing. Some learned from Native Americans which wild plants were good for eating. African Americans used creativity and hard work to make the most of their difficult circumstances.

The slave trade brought many new foods to America from Africa. Yams, okra, lima beans, licorice, and watermelon are just a few of them.

Some slaves worked in the kitchen, having to prepare food for slave owners and their families. Gradually they added African foods and recipes to the menu. Over time, African, Native American, and European influences blended into a brand new type of food: what is known today as Southern cuisine.

Black-Eyed Peas
A Good-Luck Dish

Brought from Africa, black-eyed peas are actually a bean. Typically flavored with a portion of their meat allowance, enslaved African Americans created a dish that is still a staple of the South—and will bring you good luck if you eat them on New Year's Day!

Classroom Connection Black-Eyed Peas are one of the foods that came from Africa. Do some research and make a list of other foods that are native to Africa. *[Answers will vary. Some common examples are yams, okra, lima beans, licorice, and watermelon.]*

CookingUpHistory.com

Black-Eyed Peas
1 pound black-eyed peas
4 cups water
1 medium onion
½ teaspoon salt
¼ teaspoon pepper

Wash the black-eyed peas. Place in a large pot with lid. Mix in water, onion, salt, and pepper. Simmer on top of stove for 3 to 4 hours, until the peas are soft.

Fried Okra
A Taste of Two Worlds

This dish combined a native African vegetable, okra, with slaves' allowance of cornmeal.

Classroom Connection How tall are you in feet? How tall are you in Fried Okra? Measure yourself in feet, and then see how many pieces of Fried Okra does it take to make a foot. Multiply that number by how tall you are, and now you know your height in Fried Okra! *[This activity can be performed as a class.]*

Fried Okra

CookingUpHistory.com

8 pods okra
1 cup cornmeal
1 tablespoon flour
1 teaspoon salt
½ teaspoon pepper
¼ teaspoon vegetable oil

Cut the okra into ¼ inch slices and wash them in cold water. Stir together the cornmeal, flour, salt and pepper. Roll the okra in the mixture. Fry okra in hot oil in a skillet for approximately 10 minutes, until golden brown. Drain and serve.

Fufu
An African Tradition

Fufu had long been a staple, or fundamental part, of Central and Western Africa. Displaced Africans perhaps found comfort in this food from home.

Classroom Connection Some yams from Africa look almost exactly like some sweet potatoes, which are all from the Americas. Similarly, some words sound the same, but mean very different things, like *to, too,* and *two.* These words are called *homophones.* Make a list of five pairs of homophones. *[Answers will vary. Some common homophones are the following:* see *and* sea; flour *and* flower; there, their, *and* they're; ate *and* eight.*]*

CookingUpHistory.com

Fufu

1 large yam
1 egg
5 teaspoons evaporated milk
1 small onion, grated
3 tablespoons butter
pinch of garlic salt

Peel and cut yam into small pieces. Boil in ½ cup water until soft, approximately 20 minutes. Drain and mash the yams until smooth. Mix in the egg, milk, onion, and garlic salt. Beat and roll into 2-inch balls. If the mixture is too wet, add a little flour. Fry in butter until brown.

Soldiers' Mess: The Civil War

Union and Confederate soldiers of the Civil War faced a common enemy: hunger. Although many officers dined well on food prepared for them, common soldiers had to cook their own meals from what limited rations were provided.

Mostly, soldiers were provided with flour or cornmeal, salt beef, salt pork, beans or peas, and dried fruit. Union soldiers were also issued biscuits called hardtack. These foods were chosen because they would not spoil, and so could be shipped to and carried with armies on the march.

To liven up their monotonous diets, soldiers would hunt and gather wild plants when they could. Foraging food from private homes and farms was rampant in both armies. Union soldiers could also purchase treats liked canned fruit or sugar from civilian-run shops at camps. These shopkeepers were called "sutlers."

Letters written home by both Union and Confederate soldiers often mention food—and how the soldier missed a nice home-cooked meal!

Hardtack
Watch Out for Your Teeth!

Like the Firecake of the Revolutionary War, both the North and the South provided the soldiers with a food that was filling if not tasty. Hardtack became a joke with the Union (Northern) troops, who called the biscuits "tooth dullers" and "sheet iron crackers".

Classroom Connection Hardtack had some nicknames because of how hard it is. Write a short story about how Hardtack could have gotten one of these nicknames. *[Answers will vary. Encourage student creativity.]*

CookingUpHistory.com

Hardtack
2 cups of flour
½ to ¾ cup water
1 tablespoon vegetable shortening or vegetable fat
6 pinches of salt

Mix all the ingredient together into a stiff batter. Knead several times and roll the dough out flat to ½ inch thickness on an ungreased cookie sheet. Bake for ½ hour at 400 degrees. Remove from the oven, cut dough into 3 inch squares, and punch 4 rows of holes, 4 holes per row into each square. Flip the dough over, return to oven and bake another ½ hour. Turn oven off and keep door closed. Leave dough in oven until cool.

Johnnie Cake
Better Than Hardtack?

The Johnnie Cake was a simple Southern (Confederate) meal that made use of available supplies. Some people think of it as "Confederate Hardtack."

Classroom Connection Baking soda is used in cooking to help chemical reactions take place. Try mixing together a little bit of baking soda with a little bit of vinegar. When those two meet, a chemical reaction occurs that releases a gas called carbon dioxide. Why do you think we would want gases to be released inside of bread? *[The gases released in bread make the dough rise, and make bread soft instead of being hard like a cracker.]*

Johnnie Cake

CookingUpHistory.com

2 cups cornmeal
⅔ cups milk
2 tablespoons vegetable oil
2 teaspoons baking soda
½ teaspoon salt

Mix all the ingredients together. Spoon the batter into hot cooking oil in a frying pan over a low flame. Remove and let cool.

Eggs and Bread
For a Bigger Breakfast

As the hardships of the Civil War reached the average family, stretching available food became a must. Adding breadcrumbs to eggs meant there was more breakfast available.

Classroom Connection When times are hard, people have to think of all kinds of creative ways to feed people with less food. Try to think of some other ways that people could stretch the food that they had. *[Answers will vary. Encourage student creativity.]*

CookingUpHistory.com

Eggs and Bread
½ cup breadcrumbs
2 - 3 tablespoons cream
Salt and pepper
Nutmeg
10 eggs

Combine breadcrumbs, cream, salt, pepper and nutmeg in a saucepan. Let the bread soak up all the cream. Break the eggs into it, and beat all ingredients together. Cook until eggs are done.

Idiot's Delight
Simple and Sweet

Sweet treats were popular with soldiers during the Civil War. "Idiot's Delight" used whatever fruits were available and was said to be so easy that even an "idiot" could prepare it!

Classroom Connection Most soldiers in the Civil War had to cook their own meals—even if they had spent all day marching and fighting. How might a soldier feel while cooking dinner after a battle? *[Answers will vary. Tired, hungry, relieved, etc.]*

Idiot's Delight

CookingUpHistory.com

1 cup brown sugar	4 cups water
1 cup raisins	7 tablespoons butter
1 tablespoon butter	½ cup white sugar
1 teaspoon vanilla	2 teaspoons baking powder
½ cup milk	1 cup flour

Mix together the first 5 ingredients. Bring to a boil. Combine the remaining 5 ingredients and beat into a batter. Drop the batter in a greased pan by spoonfuls. Pour first mixture over it and bake in a moderate oven at 350° until golden brown.

Foods of the Gilded Age and the Industrial Revolution

Rapid industrialization in the late 1800s transformed American eating habits. The newly wealthy began to host lavish dinner parties with fancy foods for each of twelve courses.

Machines made it easier to prepare food that was then canned. The science of pasteurization made canned food safer and greatly improved the flavor. Together these processes made it easier to mass-produce food items, which led to a great increase in the amount of new foods available.

Aiding the increase of new foods was the expansion of the railroads. Trains could move large amounts of food quickly from one place to another. Combined with new refrigerators, this meant that foods such as beef and dairy products could be brought into the city before they spoiled. Railroads also introduced the idea of "fast food"; restaurants grew up around train stops and would feed train passengers during 30-minute stops.

JELL-O
It Fits Every Mold

JELL-O, introduced in 1897, is one of the most popular mass produced foods of the time. Because of a new refining process, sugar became inexpensive in the late 1800s. Gelatin desserts were very popular and usually made into fancy shapes. Quintessentially American, JELL-O was served to immigrants on Ellis Island as a way to welcome them to the country.

Classroom Connection The Industrial Revolution changed the way people all over America could access food. Look up an invention from the time of the Industrial Revolution that made it easier for people to grow, harvest, transport, or prepare food. Write a paragraph about how this invention changed the way people ate. *[Answers will vary. Reward thoughtful responses.]*

JELL-O
CookingUpHistory.com

Use one of the original flavors, listed below, and follow the directions on the box.

- orange
- lemon
- strawberry
- raspberry

Julienne Soup
This Appetizer Will Steal the Show!

A favorite first course for the extravagant dinner parties of the newly rich industrialists of the Gilded Age, it was actually invented a century earlier by a French chef in Boston.

Classroom Connection Have every member of your class pick a favorite out of the four vegetables used in the recipe and count the number of people who choose each one. Make a bar graph that shows how many people like each flavor best. *[Ensure students label both axes.]*

CookingUpHistory.com

Julienne Soup
1 quart clear brown vegetable soup stock
¼ cup carrots, julienned
¼ cup turnips, julienned
2 tablespoons cooked peas
2 tablespoons string beans

Boil the carrots and turnips in salted water. Add in all the remaining ingredients and heat to boiling point.

Waldorf Salad
From a Five-Star Hotel to Your Kitchen

This famous dish was created by the maitre d'hotel of New York's Waldorf-Astoria hotel in 1893.

Classroom Connection Waldorf Salad takes its name from the New York Waldorf-Astoria hotel. America takes its name from someone else. Look up who America is named after and what role he played in early America. *[Amerigo Vespucci; Amerigo was an early explorer of North and South America. While he was not the first European to America, some of the first maps of the New World were based on his descriptions.]*

Waldorf Salad
CookingUpHistory.com

1 cup apples, chopped or diced (granny smith or similar sweet/tart apple)
1 tablespoon lemon juice
1 cup celery, chopped
¼ cup mayonnaise*
¼ cup raisins (optional)
¼ cup walnuts (optional - but soon added to the hotel's classic)
* yogurt may be substituted

Chop or dice the apples and sprinkle them with lemon juice. Combine with all other ingredients. Toss in a salad bowel to coat all pieces with mayonnaise. (The original was made with only diced apples, chopped celery, and mayonnaise.)

Dishes of World War I

The start of World War I changed the eating habits of Americans. Suddenly, much of the food grown in the States was needed overseas. People were asked to ration what they ate. The newly created Food Administration urged everyone to have "Wheatless Wednesdays" to free up the crop for soldiers overseas. Other days of the weeks had their own restrictions. Staples such as butter and eggs became scarce and Americans had to improvise with their food.

As the people at home learned to do without, the soldiers in Europe benefited from the hard work of the American farmer. In 1917 and 1918, U.S. farmers produced crops that were a thousand million bushels more than previous years. Most of that food was sent to soldiers fighting overseas and was a major factor in the Allied victory.

Bullets in a Pot
Don't Worry, They're Not Really Bullets!

The dried beans from American farmlands traveled far to help feed the soldiers of World War I. The beans were often served with pork.

Classroom Connection People can't eat bullets, no matter how long they're cooked. Do you think a soldier or a farmer came up with this name? Why? *[Answers will vary. Probably a soldier, since soldiers use bullets.]*

Bullets in a Pot

CookingUpHistory.com

2 lb. beans
1 cup ketchup
1 teaspoon baking soda
salt & pepper

Soak beans overnight. In the morning boil the beans and add in the baking soda. Drain thoroughly, return to pan and cover with fresh boiling water. Simmer until beans are tender, adding water as needed. Stir in the ketchup. Add salt and pepper to taste. Place in a bean pot and bake one hour at moderate temperature. If too moist, stir and bake a few minutes longer, uncovered.

Cabbage Soup
The Soldier's Soup

Cabbage soup was eaten by civilians and soldiers alike when they needed to ration their supplies. Soldiers also often had meals that were wheatless and meatless.

Classroom Connection If 12 soldiers came together to eat some Cabbage Soup, but there were only 4 bowls to eat out of, what fraction of the soldiers would have to use a helmet as a bowl? *[2/3]*

CookingUpHistory.com

Cabbage Soup

1 small head cabbage

1 cup cream

3 cups milk

salt and pepper

Chop the cabbage until very fine. It should measure about 3 cups. Cover with water in a saucepan; bring to a boil, lower heat, and simmer until tender. Drain water from cabbage, reserving 1 cup of liquid. Mix in the liquid, milk, cream, and salt and pepper to taste. Heat thoroughly, but do not boil.

1917 War Cake
A Memorable Dessert

This recipe is a prime example of improvising with what's available. Americans created this cake with no butter, no sugar, and very little flour.

Classroom Connection 1917 was an important year for America in World War I. What happened that year that changed America's involvement in the war? *[The United States declared war on Germany, entering the war.]*

1917 War Cake   CookingUpHistory.com

1 cup corn syrup	½ teaspoon nutmeg
1 cup cold water	1 tablespoon Crisco
1 teaspoon salt	1 teaspoon baking soda
½ teaspoon cloves	2 cups flour
1 teaspoon cinnamon	½ teaspoon baking powder

Combine the first 6 ingredients in a saucepan. Bring to a boil and cook for 3 more minutes. Add in the Crisco. When cool, add soda dissolved in a little hot water. Add flour and baking powder. Stir and pour into greased tube pan. Bake for 1 hour at 325 degrees.

Surviving the Great Depression

The 1930s, marked by the twin disasters of the Dust Bowl and the Great Depression, saw deep changes in the American diet.

Many of the convenience foods that had grown in popularity in the 1920s became too expensive for the average person. People drank less milk for the same reason. Fresh fruit was rare and expensive. Many families cut back to two meals a day. Those meals rarely contained meat. Soups and stews were popular because they could be stretched, and they were often made from whatever ingredients were available—even if those ingredients were weeds like dandelions and milkweed. Starvation was a real threat. Soup lines became the iconic image of the Depression.

New Deal programs helped. Cities around the country set up soup kitchens where anyone could come and have a free meal. People helped each other as well. Pot-luck suppers became popular. Small gardens were planted and the produce shared. When a family had the good fortune to have meat or extra food, neighbors were invited to the meal.

Bunny Salad
Dress-up for Food

Fruit was a rare treat for many Americans during the Great Depression. People made the most out of it. Dressing up food to make it more fun and interesting was popular during the 1930s.

Classroom Connection Why do you think people without a lot of food would dress their food up to look like rabbits? What kinds of food do we dress up today? *[Answers will vary. Reward thoughtful responses.]*

Bunny Salad   CookingUpHistory.com

Canned Pear Halves
Cottage cheese
Raisons
Slivered Almonds
Baby carrots
Lettuce

Cover the base of a plate with lettuce leaves. Place one pear half, flat side down, on the lettuce. Make ears out of the slivered almonds. Make eyes and a nose out of the raisins. Scoop a small amount of cottage cheese for the tail. Place a carrot near the bunny nose.

Meatless Meatloaf
A Tasty Way to Do Without

Many Americans lived on a meatless diet during the Great Depression—they simply could not afford not to. This "meatloaf" was one way they coped.

Classroom Connection Cut a piece of Meatless Meatloaf in the shape of a cube. How many sides does the piece of meatloaf have? How many corners? How many edges? *[6, 8, 12]*

CookingUpHistory.com

Meatless Meatloaf

1 cup rice
1 cup peanuts, crushed
1 cup cottage cheese
1 egg
1 tablespoon oil
1 teaspoon salt

Mix all the ingredients together. Bake in a loaf pan for 30 minutes or until loaf is good and set.

Creamed Peas on Toast
A Homegrown Meal

Growing your own peas and making your own bread meant that you could provide a good meal for your family.

Classroom Connection What was Black Tuesday? What happened? *[October 24, 1929; stock prices plummeted to a degree that would not be seen again for nearly 40 years; Black Tuesday signaled the beginning of the Great Depression.]*

Creamed Peas on Toast

CookingUpHistory.com

2 cups frozen green peas, thawed
⅔ cups water
⅛ teaspoon salt
3 tablespoons butter
⅓ cup heavy cream
2 tablespoons all purpose flour
1 tablespoon sugar

Place the peas, water, and salt in a medium saucepan. Bring to a boil, then mix in the butter. In a small bowl, whisk together cream, flour, and sugar. Stir this mixture into the peas. Cook over medium-high heat until thick and bubbly, about 5 minutes. Serve on toast.

Foods of World War II

Food was rationed by the government during World War II. Families received books of ration coupons to use to purchase sugar, butter, coffee, cheese, meat, canned goods, and other staples. The purpose of rationing was twofold: to ensure soldiers had enough to eat and to ensure scarce foodstuffs were distributed fairly among on the home front.

Victory gardens—home vegetable gardens planted to increase the food supply—were extremely popular. By 1945 there were 20 million victory gardens in the United States, and they provided nearly half of the country's vegetables.

American service members lived and fought in diverse environments all over the world. As a result, their diets varied tremendously. However, one iconic American foodstuff from World War II was the "C-Ration." The C-Ration was intended to be used by troops when fresh food or uncooked food was unavailable or impractical. Although contents evolved during the course of the war, a typical C-Ration included a 12-ounce canned, precooked entrée (e.g., Meat Stew with Vegetables, Frankfurters and Beans). A second can contained crackers, sugar tablets, candy, and a powdered beverage mix (e.g., coffee or lemonade). Rounding out the C-Ration was a paper-wrapped accessory pack that contained sugar and salt tablets, a spoon, chewing gum, cigarettes and matches, toilet paper, and a can opener.

Potato Floddie
Tastes like... Victory!

Growing your own potatoes in your victory garden meant that you could provide a tasty, filling meal without worrying about rationed food.

Classroom Connection Many types of food and supplies were rationed as part of the war effort in World War II. What do you think was rationed, and why? *[Answers will vary. The following were rationed: tires, cars, bicycles, gasoline, fuel oil, kerosene, solid fuels, stoves, typewriters, shoes, sugar, processed food, meat, cheese, canned milk, and canned fish, fats.]*

Potato Floddie

CookingUpHistory.com

2 potatoes
2 oz. flour
⅓ cup water
salt and pepper, to taste
vegetable shortening
pinch of mixed herbs

Clean the potatoes and grate with a coarse grater over a bowl (do not peel — wasteful). Add the flour and water to form a batter. Season with salt and pepper. Heat dripping/lard/oil until hot in frying pan. Drop the mixture into the pan. When brown on one side, flip and brown the other. Serve with jam for a sweet dish, or for something savory, add a pinch of herbs and another dash of pepper.

Syrup Loaf
Not Your Ordinary Bread

Rationing proved to be no problem for creative cooks; this bread has no sugar or eggs.

Classroom Connection During World War II, many women took on the jobs of soldiers who had gone to war. A series of famous posters depicted "Rosie the Riveter." What would have happened if these women had simply stayed at home? *[Answers will vary, and should reflect an understanding of the vital role women played in winning the war. Reward thoughtful responses.]*

CookingUpHistory.com

Syrup Loaf
4 oz. self-rising flour or plain flour with 2 teaspoons baking powder
½ teaspoon of bicarbonate of soda (baking soda)
pinch of salt
2 tablespoons warmed golden syrup
¼ of a pint of milk

Sift flour, (or flour and baking powder), bicarbonate of soda and salt. Heat the syrup and milk, pour over the flour and beat well. Pour into a greased 1 lb. loaf tin and bake in the center of a moderately hot oven for 30 minutes or until firm.

Honey Cake
It's the Bee's Knees!

Dessert is always a favorite dish. During World War II, when sugar was scarce, this cake was made with honey.

Classroom Connection Find a picture of a honeycomb. What shapes do you see? Why is this a good shape for a honeycomb? *[Hexagons; hexagons can stack on top of one another without wasting any space.]*

Honey Cake

CookingUpHistory.com

½ cup solid vegetable shortening
1 cup honey
1 egg, well beaten
2 cups flour
1 teaspoon baking soda

½ teaspoon salt
½ teaspoon cinnamon
½ cup sour milk (½ cup milk mixed with ½ teaspoon white vinegar)

Cream the shortening in a bowl with honey and egg. In separate bowl, sift together flour, baking soda, salt, and cinnamon. Add the 2 above alternately, with sour milk, to shortening mixture. Spread the batter into a greased and floured 13x9 inch baking ban. Smooth top of batter with spatula. Bake in 350 degree oven for 35 minutes.

American Fare: the 1950s

The 1950s were an era of prosperity for America. New foods and new technology completely changed the way Americans ate and the kind of foods they ate.

Packaged, prepared foods grew in popularity. Packaged foods brought Americans together in a new way. Instead of eating traditional, regional foods, cooks began preparing meals from the back of boxes so families everywhere were eating the same foods for dinner.

Packaged foods, like canned soups and frozen vegetables, brought about one of the most popular foods of the 1950s—casseroles. This combination of veggies and meat, bound together with a soup base and baked in the oven graced the dinner tables of numerous households. Backyard barbecues were also an important part of the American diet of the 1950s.

Mac 'n' Cheese
Cheesy Classic!

The 1950s was the decade of comfort foods. The Great Depression and World War II had left Americans with the desire to fill their plates and their stomachs with good food. This recipe is a classic comfort food and still very popular today.

Classroom Connection Mac 'n' Cheese is a food that many Americans have made from a box. Notice how much better it is made from scratch! What other foods from a box would you like to try to make from scratch? *[Answers will vary.]*

Mac 'n' Cheese
CookingUpHistory.com

1 8 oz. package elbow macaroni	1 ¼ tablespoon dry mustard
¾ cups fresh bread crumbs	1 teaspoon salt
4 tablespoons butter, melted	⅛ teaspoon pepper
1 small onion, finely chopped	1 ½ cups milk
1 tablespoon all purpose flour	8 oz. cheddar cheese, shredded

Cook and drain macaroni. Preheat oven to 350°. Grease baking dish. In a small bowl, toss breadcrumbs and 2 tablespoons melted butter until moistened. Set aside. In saucepan, melt 2 tablespoons butter over medium heat. Add onion and cook until tender, about 5 minutes. Mix in flour, mustard, salt, and pepper. Blend. Stir in milk. Cook, stir, until thickened. Remove from heat, stir in cheese. Spoon macaroni into baking dish. Pour cheese sauce over macaroni. Sprinkle crumb mixture over top. Bake until top is golden, about 20 minutes.

California Dip
Delicious in Any State

This simple dish quickly became a sensation in the 1950s. Legend has it that California Dip was invented by a housewife in California. Perhaps. But the recipe appeared on onion soup mixes in households across the country.

Classroom Connection There are lots of different dip recipes. Imagine you had a dip contest to try to determine the best one. You picked out 12 different judges. 12 different people made their favorite dip and brought enough for each judge to have one sample. How many samples would there be in all? *[144]*

CookingUpHistory.com

California Dip

1 envelope dry onion soup mix

2 cups sour cream

Mix the ingredients and chill several hours to combine the flavors.
Serve with potato chips, crackers, or raw vegetables.

Red Hot Salad
An Unconventional Salad

Like teenagers today, teenagers of the 1950s enjoyed getting together for parties. Gathering to listen to music and dance always included food. Using packaged foods made this recipe easy enough for the teenagers to make themselves.

Classroom Connection Have students ask appropriate adults to tell them stories about life during the 1950s. *[Stories will vary.]*

Red Hot Salad

CookingUpHistory.com

6 oz. cherry JELL-O
4 oz. red hots candy
3 cups boiling water
20 oz. pineapple, crushed, undrained
2 cups applesauce

Dissolve the JELL-O and red hots in boiling water. Add the pineapple and applesauce once the mixture has cooled to room temperature. Pour into oiled 8 cup mold and chill until set.

Vanilla Milkshake
"I'm All Shook Up"

The 1950s saw the rise of fast food restaurants. A burger and fries served with a milkshake was standard fare as the restaurants spread across the country.

Classroom Connection Use a ruler to measure the different tools that get ice cream to your stomach. How long is the ice cream scoop? How long is your spoon? How long is your arm? How far is it from your mouth to your stomach? *[Ensure students use rulers properly.]*

CookingUpHistory.com

Vanilla Milkshake
4 scoops vanilla ice cream
1 tablespoon vanilla extract
1 ½ cups milk

Put into a blender and blend until smooth.
Serve immediately.

Popular Dishes of the 1960s

Some of the food changes of the 1960s came from celebrities. First Lady Jacqueline Kennedy popularized elaborate dinners. Soon people across America were preparing and enjoying their own fancy dinner parties. In 1963, Julia Child debuted her enormously popular cooking show, and French cooking became the rage.

Not all of the changes were in fine dining. Vegetarianism gained popularity as part of the new trend in healthy eating. Frieda Caplan, a produce entrepreneur, brought exotic fruits, like mangos and kiwis, to the American dinner table. Salad bars started showing up in restaurants. People grew more interested in authentic ethnic foods. Fast food restaurants continued their growth across the country, and new junk foods were introduced.

Eating in all parts of the world became more important to Americans as world hunger became a focus. Improved varieties of seeds for wheat, corn, and rice were developed. These new varieties allowed farmers to produce more crops in the same amount of space. These seeds were shared with other countries in an effort to end world hunger.

Potato Salad
A Lunchbox Favorite!

Potatoes, native to the New World, were introduced to Europe by Spanish explorers. It was there, probably in Germany and probably in the 1500s, that the type of potato salad we are familiar with originated. European settlers brought their recipes to America. In the 1960s, potato salad was standard fare in students' lunchboxes.

Classroom Connection What are some advantages and disadvantages to taking your lunch to school or work, instead of buying it someplace? *[Answers will vary. Advantages: get to pack what you want; more nutritious. Disadvantages: might have to find a refrigerator; might miss a good meal.]*

CookingUpHistory.com

Potato Salad

5 potatoes
3 eggs
1 cup chopped celery
½ cup chopped onion
½ cup sweet pickle relish

¼ teaspoon garlic salt
¼ teaspoon celery salt
1 tablespoon prepared mustard
ground black pepper to taste
¼ cup mayonnaise

Bring a large pot of salted water to a boil. Cook potatoes until tender (about 15 minutes.) Drain the potatoes and let cool. Peel and chop. Cover eggs in a saucepan with cold water. Bring water to a boil. Cover and remove from heat. Let eggs stand in hot water for 10 minutes. Remove from hot water and let cool. Peel and chop. In a large bowl, combine all of the ingredients. Mix together well. Cover and refrigerate. Serve chilled.

Cheese Fondue
Let's Take a Dip

During the 1960s, dishes that used an open flame or burning for a spectacular finish became popular at many dinner parties and restaurants. Fondue soon became a favorite.

Classroom Connection Where does the word "fondue" come from? *[from the French, "to melt" (cheese!)]*

Cheese Fondue

CookingUpHistory.com

2 cups shredded Swiss cheese
2 cups shredded Gruyere cheese
2 tablespoons flour
1 clove garlic, cut in half
1 tablespoon lemon juice

Mix the cheeses with flour in a large bowl, being sure the cheese is thoroughly coated. Rub garlic on the bottom and sides of the fondue dish and discard. Pour broth into fondue dish and heat just until bubbles rise to the surface. Stir in lemon juice. Gradually add the cheese, about ½ cup at a time, stirring constantly over low heat, until cheeses are melted. Add more cheese, if needed, to reach desired thickness. Serve immediately.

Tomato Delight
Nice and Light

Finding vegetarian meals today is relatively easy. Even mainstream grocery stores carry a variety of vegetarian foods beyond fruits and vegetables. This was not true in the 1960s. Vegetarians had to search out their own recipes, like this one.

Classroom Connection There are lots of different reasons why people are vegetarians. Talk with some vegetarians you know and do some research to learn more about why some people don't eat meat. *[Typically, vegetarians are vegetarian for their health or because they oppose hurting animals.]*

CookingUpHistory.com

Tomato Delight

3 ripe tomatoes, thinly sliced
1 Vidalia onion, thinly sliced
1 clove garlic, minced
⅓ cup balsamic vinegar
⅓ cup olive oil
1 tablespoon dried basil
1 tablespoon marjoram
⅛ teaspoon coriander seeds
⅛ teaspoon dried mint
1 teaspoon dried oregano
3 tablespoons sugar
1 teaspoon salt
1 teaspoon pepper

In a bowl, combine vinegar and olive oil. Whisk vigorously. Stir in spices, salt, pepper and sugar. Continue to whisk until emulsified. Pour some of the vinaigrette into a glass dish. Add a layer of tomatoes and a layer of onion. Sprinkle with salt and pepper. Add vinaigrette. Repeat until vegetables are used. Finish with vinaigrette. Cover with plastic wrap. Refrigerate for 2 hours.

Recipes of the 1970s

Small appliance technology boomed in the 1970s. Cuisinart marketed the first food processor. This little machine was a revolution in the kitchen. Cooks everywhere could now chop, mix, and puree with ease, creating dishes that were impractical, if not impossible, beforehand. Crock-Pot released their slow cooker, allowing busy families to come home to a fully cooked meal.

Perhaps the most influential cooking technology of the decade was the microwave oven. While home models were available as early as the 1950s, they were large and expensive. Technological innovation reduced both size and price, and by 1975 microwave ovens were outselling electric ovens. The kitchen hasn't been the same since.

In the 1970s, people became increasingly concerned about chemicals and pesticides used on farms. The idea of organic food—food grown and prepared with no artificial chemicals—gained popularity.

Alice Waters opened a restaurant in Berkeley, California, called Chez Panisse. It featured local, organic, seasonal foods. Known as California Cuisine, this style of cooking spread across America.

Cucumber, Mango, and Red Onion Salad
A Feast for the Eyes

In the 1970s, increasing numbers of health-conscious Americans sought food grown without artificial fertilizers or pesticides. This salad shows that simple, natural foods can be both satisfying to the eye as well as the appetite.

Classroom Connection What does *organic* mean? Write a paragraph on why some people prefer organic food over others. *[Organic foods are grown and prepared without any chemicals or pesticides. Paragraphs will vary. Reward thoughtful responses.]*

CookingUpHistory.com

Cucumber, Mango, and Red Onion Salad
1 medium cucumber, peeled and thinly sliced
1 mango, pitted and cut into large dice
1 red onion, sliced into thin rounds
2 tablespoons lime juice
salt to taste
3 tablespoons cilantro

Slice then combine the cucumber, mango, and red onion in medium bowl. Season to taste with lime juice and salt. Garnish generously with cilantro leaves.

Deviled Eggs
Surprisingly Heavenly

Deviled eggs were not invented in the 1970s, but they graced many American tables (including picnic tables!) during that decade. (They were originally a picnic treat . . . in Ancient Rome!)

Classroom Connection Take a hard-boiled egg and an uncooked egg. Try to spin them on a large table. Which one is easier to spin? Why do you think this is so? *[Hard-boiled eggs are easier to spin because the liquid yolk of a raw egg moves around inside the raw egg white.]*

Deviled Eggs   CookingUpHistory.com

6 large hard boiled eggs
3 tablespoons mayonnaise
1 tablespoon sugar
1 teaspoon mustard
1 teaspoon vinegar
salt & pepper to taste
paprika (optional)

After boiling the eggs, break off the shells. Slice the eggs in half lengthwise.
Carefully scoop out the yolks. Mix the yolks and remaining ingredients.
Carefully spoon mixture back into the egg white halves.
Garnish with a light sprinkling of paprika, if desired.

Lucy Lemon Squares
Yummy No Matter What Shape They Take

The desire for dessert never changes. This version of an old favorite was developed in 1975.

Classroom Connection Cut the Lemon Squares into a bunch of different shapes. Take two triangle shaped pieces and put them together to form a square. What other shapes can you combine to make different shapes? *[Answers will vary. Encourage student creativity.]*

CookingUpHistory.com

Lucy Lemon Squares

Crust:
1 cup flour
½ cup butter
¼ cup powdered sugar

Filling:
2 eggs
1 cup sugar
½ teaspoon baking powder
2 ½ tablespoons fresh lemon juice
dash of salt

Crust: Sift flour and sugar into bowl. Mix in the butter until well mixed. Spread evenly on the bottom of an 8x8 inch baking pan. Bake for 20 minutes at 350 degrees.

Filling: Beat all ingredients together. Pour over the baked crust and place all in the oven for 20-25 minutes. Cool on rack. Cut in squares. Sprinkle with sifted, powdered sugar.

Some Current Treats

Early Native Americans and colonists could never have dreamed of the stunning variety and tremendous quantity of food available in the United States today. Food from all over the world is part of the American diet. American food diversity reflects Americans' diversity.

Despite this diversity, Americans too often make unhealthy food decisions, turning to the convenience of fast food and junk food. This has caused an increase in obesity across the nation.

But there are positive signs. Demands for healthier choices in fast foods grow greater each year. More people are purchasing and eating locally grown fruits and vegetables. Information on foods and their nutritional content is easily available. Many fast food restaurants now offer salads and low-fat meals. The message of eating in moderation is gaining traction.

The United States is a product of the people who live here. People from all over the world have come to this country to begin new lives. Each of them brought pieces of their old lives with them, and those little pieces included their food. Over 500 years of new people, ideas, and foods have created not only a unique country, but also an amazing place to eat!

Trail Mix
Go Ahead, Take a Hike!

Today more people are choosing to eat healthy foods. Full of fruits and nuts, this snack is healthy and it represents the diversity of foods available in America.

Classroom Connection Trail Mix is a wonderful snack because you can make it whatever way you like best. Pick your favorite five ingredients from the list. Using twelfths, show what part of the whole you would like each ingredient to make up. *[Answers will vary, but student responses should add up to twelve twelfths.]*

CookingUpHistory.com

Trail Mix
¼ cup of each of the following ingredients:

unsalted peanuts	chocolate chips
sunflower seeds	pretzels
dried cranberries	cheerios
dried cherries	chex
dried apricots	granola
raisins	

Mix together in a bowl, omitting any ingredient you dislike. Store in an airtight container or serve immediately.

Yogurt Parfait
Good, and Good For Ya!

Healthy eating doesn't mean you have to skip dessert—just make sure it's delicious *and* nutritious like this parfait.

Classroom Connection Like a lot of our foods, we keep yogurt in a refrigerator to keep bacteria from growing in it. Do you know how cold a refrigerator should be? *[40°F or below]*

Yogurt Parfait

CookingUpHistory.com

plain, low fat yogurt
bananas
berries
crushed graham crackers
nuts
flavored granola

Crush the berries and bananas then mix them with yogurt. Layer your favorite ingredients with the yogurt, until glass is full.

Monkey Bread
So Tasty, it's Bananas!

Eating healthy means eating the right size portion. Particularly with desserts, this is something to remember.

Classroom Connection How do people know what the right size portion is? How do we know how to eat enough, but not too much? *[Answers will vary. There are many techniques to use: feeling full, keeping track of calories, following specific diets, and so on.]*

CookingUpHistory.com

Monkey Bread

4 cans refrigerated biscuits

1 cup packed brown sugar

1 ½ sticks butter (¾ cup)

½ cup white sugar

2 tablespoons cinnamon

Preheat oven to 350 degrees. Grease a 9-10 inch tube pan. Shake together the white sugar and cinnamon in medium plastic bag. Cut biscuits into halves or quarters. Place six to eight biscuit pieces in sugar cinnamon mix. Shake well. Put the pieces in the bottom of greased pan. Continue layering until all the biscuit pieces are coated and in the pan. In a small saucepan, melt the butter with the brown sugar over medium heat. Boil for one minute. Pour this mixture over layered biscuits. Bake for 35 minutes. Let cool in pan for 10 minutes, then turn out onto a plate.

Printed in Germany
by Amazon Distribution
GmbH, Leipzig